HERONS

First published in Great Britain in 1993 by
Colin Baxter Photography Ltd.,
Grantown on Spey,
Morayshire, PH26 3NA,
Scotland

British Library Cataloguing in Publication Data
Mick Marquiss
Herons
I. Title
598.34

ISBN 0-948661-29-1

Photography copyright © 1993 by

Front Cover © Nigel Dennis (NHPA)
Back Cover © Laurie Campbell
Page 19 © Manfred Danegger (NHPA)
Page 20 © E & D Hosking (FLPA)
Page 21 © Dr K Day
Page 22 © John Clarke
Page 23 © Laurie Campbell
Page 24 © Laurie Campbell
Page 25 Top © Laurie Campbell
Page 25 Bottom © Steve Cooper
Page 26 © Laurie Campbell
Page 27 © Jim Young
Page 28 © Laurie Campbell
Page 29 © Laurie Campbell

Page 30 © Laurie Campbell
Page 35 © Laurie Campbell
Page 36 © Nigel Dennis (NHPA)
Page 37 © Laurie Campbell
Page 38 © Laurie Campbell
Page 39 © Laurie Campbell
Page 40 © Stan Osolinski (Oxford Scientific Films)
Page 41 © Colin Baxter
Page 42 © Carol Hughes (Bruce Coleman)
Page 43 © Niall Benvie
Page 44 © Laurie Campbell
Page 45 © Laurie Campbell
Page 46 © Laurie Campbell

Heron Illustration © Keith Brockie

Printed in Great Britain by
Frank Peters Printers Ltd., Kendal.

HERONS

Mick Marquiss

Colin Baxter Photography Ltd., Grantown-on-Spey, Scotland

Grey Herons

Even those who know very little about birds can recognise a heron instantly for it is unmistakable - a large bird standing about a metre high, with long legs, long neck, a slim head and a dagger-shaped bill. It is just as characteristic in flight. The head and neck are retracted, but the wings are broad and rounded, and the legs held out behind. The wings beat slowly, almost leisurely, and the flight often ends with a prolonged descent, gliding on slightly decurved wings prior to landing. Perhaps most striking are the calls of herons: a loud shriek from a bird flying overhead at night, the grunting of a bird approaching its nest, or the cacophony of snaps, pops, yelps and growls that emanate from the midst of a breeding colony.

The heron most familiar to people in Britain is properly called the grey heron. Weighing in at between 1.3 and 2 kilograms, it is the largest member of the heron family (*Ardeidae*) in Europe. It also has the most northerly distribution, its geographical range extending from Western Europe to India, south into Africa, and north as far as Finland. Most European members of the family (which includes herons, egrets, night herons and bitterns) are birds of shallow water habitats, feeding on fish or large invertebrates. At higher latitudes such habitats are increasingly liable to freeze over in winter so these birds are summer migrants. Only in the more amenable climes of southern Europe can they be year-round residents. Most grey herons are able to survive moderate winters, but those which breed in Eastern Europe and as far north as Norway, Sweden or Finland, migrate south or west for the winter. Scotland supports a resident population of herons because the generally milder winters and the seashores warmed by the Gulf

Stream provide sufficient winter habitat to sustain a large number of birds. In North America there is the slightly larger great blue heron, which is also migratory in the north of its range, only a small number spending the winter as far north as British Columbia or the Canadian Maritime Provinces. Scotland is thus probably unique in supporting the most northerly resident population of any heron species in the world.

Both the grey heron's English and Latin (*Ardea cinerea*) names are aptly descriptive because it is a predominantly grey (cinereous) bird. On adults the upper-parts are grey, although the head, much of the neck, and the breast are white. The large wing feathers are dark blue-grey and the tail feathers paler grey. Black feathers above and behind the eye create a striking head pattern which extends backwards to the nape where two long trailing feathers adorn an erectile crest. There are black centres to some neck feathers creating a line of broken chevrons down the front. An inky black patch below the white breast extends to the sides of the belly and up either side of the chest to be exposed as smart epaulettes above the folded wing joint, contrasting with the white leading edges of the wings. The feathers of the lower back and those that hang over the folded wings are elongated with loose tips which form short pearly-grey plumes. Longer white plumes hang from the lower breast. For most of the year the eyes and bill are yellow and the legs olive-brown. In spring, with the onset of nuptial display, the upper legs and the bill turn pink; this verges on orange in some individuals though the colour fades rapidly as breeding proceeds.

Grey herons in their first year have dull grey plumage above, paler below and on their face, unrelieved except for the neckline of darker grey or black, broken chevrons and a dark cap. The bill is grey with a dull yellow lower mandible. Some of the nape, back and breast feathers are long but not long enough to form plumes. Some young birds have buff fringes to their feathers which can make them appear brown, and occasionally individual birds can look quite dusky. All herons have three sets of feather tracts which continually produce dense, brittle feathers which break up to form a fine powder. These patches of yellow 'powder down' are on the sides of the breast, the lower back (sacrum), and the groin, and act as dusting sites for use during preening. The bird rubs and shakes its head, neck and wings in these patches to cover its feathers with dust which is then shaken and combed from the plumage using the bill and feet. To this end the inner edge of the claw on the middle toe of each foot is serrated to comb the feathers as the foot passes over them. This process is particularly effective in removing the slime which is often liberally deposited on the head and neck feathers of herons as they kill and manipulate eels prior to swallowing them.

The striking appearance of adult herons is used in signalling. The pink colouring of the bill and legs is a good indication of a bird's physiological state - its readiness for breeding. A male grey heron will advertise his position on a potential nest site by 'flashing' at passing birds. He erects his throat and breast feathers, outlined by the adjacent black feathers to produce a flash of white as his head and neck are stretched upwards and backwards. This is accompanied by a peculiar grating noise, alternating with single, but very loud, shrieks. With such an exhibition, a male bird cannot help but be noticed. The raising of crest feathers is frequent whenever herons meet. It emphasises the head and bill and is thought to convey mood, in particular aggression, because it accompanies threatening postures and often precedes an attack - a lunge with the bill. Male and female herons have very similar plumage, the only obvious difference being that the male has distinctly longer plumes. In contrast, young herons are dowdy with no ornamental plumage, presumably because, they are rarely involved in the sorts of signalling required for breeding and their best interests, at least initially, are served by remaining discreet. The pattern of broken chevrons on the young bird's neck is the most obvious plumage feature but this is probably useful in foraging because, by disrupting the outline of the neck, the bird is less easily seen by fish.

Young birds start to replace their body feathers in their first autumn, and flight feathers the following summer. Adult birds moult their feathers from May to July but do not replace all of them within one year. Flight feathers are shed sequentially from the middle of the wing outwards, stopping at the end of the moult period, often having only replaced a few large feathers. The following May wing moult starts from where it had stopped, but also recommences from the middle of the wing, so that two waves of moulting feathers proceed outwards. Before the outermost wing feathers are finally shed, most birds have initiated a third wave. In this way herons can replace several wing feathers simultaneously whilst avoiding large gaps in the wing, which could severely handicap their flight.

I assume that herons are such a characteristic shape because it helps them earn their living by catching fish in shallow water. Their long legs and toes enable them to stand and wade in water, often up to half a metre deep, and their long neck gives them the reach to strike at prey. Their eyes are set wide apart and can be directed forwards to provide binocular vision, enabling a heron to judge distance. The eyes can also be directed downwards so that they can scan an area both ahead of, and below the bill, whilst keeping the head motionless. The bill itself is long and pointed to give the combination of precision and grip required to seize, hold and manipulate slippery fish. The process of catching a fish begins with the heron standing or slowly walking in the water, peering intently ahead. Once the prey is sighted the heron's body moves slowly forward while the neck is retracted and the head lowered until the bill is close to the water's surface. The fish is attacked with a single lunge, the kinked neck straightening at speed to catapult the head into the water. Most fish are seized between the mandibles : very few are actually pierced, even by one mandible, the fish being gripped rather than skewered. Once caught, the fish has to be manipulated in the bill; the heron tossing or shaking it until it can be turned and swallowed head first.

To catch fish in this manner is not quite so straightforward as it seems and there are apparently some tricks of the trade that herons need to learn. When flying into a fishing site, they seem to prefer to land out of the water and wade in - a walk in probably disturbs fish less than a splash landing. I am told that herons leave the water to defecate. Although I have not seen this myself I can believe that fish might be wary of an odorous white streak in the water. Herons see fish through the water's surface and must take account of refraction in judging the precise position and depth of a fish and thus where to strike. Furthermore, a fish seized in the area between the gills and the widest part of the body is less likely to wriggle free than one gripped elsewhere. As a young man I spent hours catching flounders by feeling for them in the mud with my feet, then lifting them out by hand into a shoulder bag. If you grip a flounder's gill covers tightly between thumb and forefinger the fish will remain limp and can be smoothly lifted from the sea. Grip it anywhere else and it is sure to be lost !

If a heron catches a fish that struggles and requires prolonged handling it usually walks or flies ashore before starting to manipulate it, so that a dropped fish does not result in the loss of a meal. Also brought ashore are very large or awkwardly-shaped fish. For instance, on capture long-spined sea scorpions (granny fish) blow themselves rigid so that their spines stick out, and they require some pecking and shaking to kill and relax them before they can be consumed. Almost all eels are brought ashore to be pecked around the head and killed, or at least subdued, prior to swallowing. A freshly caught eel will wrap itself into coils around the bill, head and neck of the heron and even if the bird manages to get it down head first, a lively eel can double up on itself in the gullet, so that the bird has to swallow faster than the eel can swim to prevent it snaking back out of its mouth. A heron must also be able to judge the size of a fish, as there would be no point in catching a fish too big to swallow.

Much of this fishing skill must be learned by experience and I have frequently watched juvenile herons breaking the rules. They seem to be impatient and splash unnecessarily. They often strike at sticks or weed and sometimes catch fish by the tail, or fumble during manipulation so that it is dropped back into the water. They waste precious fishing time on the rising tide by spending ten to fifteen minutes trying to manipulate a flounder which is far too big for them to eat. I have rarely seen an adult bird do any of these things.

Grey herons are the least specialised of European herons and their diet is as variable as the habitats they frequent. They can feed in almost any shallow water habitat containing fish, including rocky seashores, estuaries, lochs and marshes, rivers and streams, tiny ditches, garden ponds and fish farms. In early spring they eat a lot of frogs and in the uplands at that time of year they can be found peering into the peaty pools of sphagnum bogs. I have also seen them in dry habitats looking for other prey - stalking voles in rough pastures, and walking in the furrows of a newly ploughed field eating earthworms. I once saw a heron staring intently into the grass on the wide verge of a motorway apparently oblivious of the passing traffic. I have also seen an adult bird pecking at a rabbit carcass at the side of the road in late winter. Perhaps this bird was short of food, but herons regularly take dead fish from fish farm dumps, and those on the Scottish river Dee scavenge the carcasses of spent kelts (salmon) after spawning, so they do not always require live food. However, for most of the year the majority of herons get their food by fishing in the shallows.

The types of fish eaten by herons vary according to their fishing sites. In the uplands the birds frequent burns or streams so their diet is almost entirely small trout between five and eighteen centimetres, with a few lampreys, frogs and voles according to season. At slightly lower altitudes, where there are wider river sections, juvenile salmon are consumed and the trout tend to be larger - up to twenty-two centimetres. However, the most outstanding feature here is the large numbers of eels taken in June and July. On rivers such as the Tweed and the Tay in Scotland, eels can make up more than half of the fish consumed in those months. Herons feeding on the lowest reaches of rivers have a more diverse diet, including roach, grayling, flounder and, on the river Annan, for example the occasional chub. Loch margins provide perch, three-spined sticklebacks and sometimes roach, water voles or mallard ducklings. Herons feeding on the coast have the greatest variety of fishes available to them and their diet varies accordingly. Estuarine feeders take huge numbers of three-spined sticklebacks and shrimps, but the bulk of fish flesh they consume comes from flounders three to seventeen centimetres long. Rocky-shore feeders also take a large number of small items including lots of prawns, but mainly seaweed fishes such as long-spined sea scorpions, fifteen-spined sticklebacks, butterfish and wrasse. In the late summer their intake can be boosted substantially with small eels and, in some years, an abundance of young saithe (coalfish).

From this brief description of their diet it might seem that herons benefit from a superabundance of prey and can pick and choose to suit their palate, but this is certainly not the case. In any one place and at any one time one particular type of prey will be the most easily captured. Variety in the diet probably reflects both the diversity of habitats and changes in the availability of particular prey from day to day or week to week. Alan Leitch and I looked in depth at the diet of herons breeding near Loch Leven in Fife from 1981 to 1983. At that time there seemed to be two main feeding habitats represented, with the young at some nests being fed almost wholly on small trout from burns whilst those at other nests were fed on a variety of foods from the lochside. Yet at any one time the diet of this second group of nestlings was not particularly diverse. It was dominated by field voles and frogs in March, perch in April and early May, and small ducklings in late May and June, with a mixture of items thereafter. Perch were the best food because they were the largest items; nutritious mature fish which came into the shallow water to spawn in April. Although small mallard ducklings were also available in April - several thousands hatch at Loch Leven most years - they were not taken by herons until the perch had finished spawning and departed into deep water. As ducklings became less abundant the diet switched again, this time to tiny sticklebacks and other items. These observations lead me to believe that herons have a restricted choice of feeding sites and that changes in their diet are due to a decline in the availability of the most nourishing (generally the biggest !) items.

A study by Heinz Richner, on the Ythan estuary and some adjacent freshwater streams, quantified the feeding rates of herons in winter showing that they varied from place to place and time to time, and that herons reacted accordingly. Some herons fed only on streams where their food intake rate was fairly constant throughout the day and adequate to sustain them. Other birds, on the estuary, only fed there three hours either side of low tide, a period when they had very good foraging success. As the tide rose and their food intake declined, they switched to feed at stream sites. The birds switching between habitats seemed to be better off because in midwinter they were half a kilogram heavier than those feeding only on freshwater sites. Most of these herons aggressively defended their feeding sites, at least when they were using them. I presume there were insufficient estuarine feeding sites to enable all the herons in the area to adopt the lucrative 'switching' strategy.

This study is important because it offers an explanation for what happens elsewhere. Some feeding sites are occupied consistently by herons and are rigorously defended. Even after they have had their daily ration, some birds stand within view of their patch and chase off any other heron which tries to use it. In contrast, there are some apparently quite productive feeding sites which are only used intermittently and remain undefended when a bird is not actually fishing. It may be that only those sites which are consistently and highly productive are seen as worth defending. Unproductive places require no defence, and a bird that switches between sites cannot keep a twenty-four hour watch on any one site.

Young birds are less adept at fishing and so are less well fed than adults. They are lighter in weight, on average, and tend to be subordinate in disputes with adults. As a result they are at a disadvantage in the competition for the best fishing places.

Most of them probably get by, but with a shaky repertoire of poor foraging sites which predisposes them to food shortages if the weather changes for the worse.

In autumn, as the weather gets colder, many freshwater fish stop feeding and move into deeper water. Some bury themselves deep in the stones and sediment in the stream bed and do not emerge until the temperature rises again in spring. This means that in winter some heron feeding sites become unproductive and, if the weather becomes severe, ice or drifting snow can cover the remainder. In autumn there is a general exodus of herons from the uplands, towards the coast where feeding sites are still tenable. There is naturally, intense competition for such sites and the more severe the winter, the more likely are young herons to find themselves short of food. The overwinter mortality of juvenile herons in Britain is correlated with winter temperatures - over eighty percent may survive the mildest of winters but it is thought that almost none came through the prolonged severe weather of 1962/63. Very cold weather seems to affect adult herons far less, particularly those which breed on the coast. Birds which feed on the rocky shores of sheltered sea-lochs may use their feeding sites year round.

This does not necessarily ensure them an easy life because shore feeding has its own particular problems. In theory seashore sites could provide sufficient food to sustain a heron every day of the year, but they can only be used at low tide, which places an upper limit on the amount of food that can be taken from them. To breed successfully one or other of a pair of herons must attend the nest to keep the eggs warm and the young safe. This means that during moonless nights, when only one low tide period is available each day, one of the pair must find an alternative food supply or go hungry. In places on the west coast of Scotland, where freshwater feeding sites are scarce, breeding herons have a high failure rate, with many unhatched eggs and very small broods of young. I suspect many shore-feeding herons may live long but unproductive lives.

Grey herons are monogamous and most breed in colonies which, for instance in France and Greece can contain up to several hundred pairs, though heronries of this size are rare in Britain. In Scotland only two colonies have numbered fifty pairs or more in recent years, and about a quarter of nesting places only harbour one or two pairs. Nests are usually in places inaccessible to ground predators, mainly in trees but sometimes on cliffs or even on the ground, on islets in lochs. In the Hebrides there are odd nests built on croft or bothy ruins, on islands where there are no trees or suitable cliffs. The nests themselves are large flat platforms up to a metre across, built of sticks, most of which have been gleaned from the ground or from adjacent unused (or at least unguarded) nests. Many nests are used year after year and become consolidated, bulky structures.

Herons sometimes return to colonies to begin courtship display in January but, in Scotland most activity does not commence until late February. Males occupy existing old platforms, or perch on potential nest sites, displaying their plumes and calling to repel males and attract females. At first all birds, male and female, are chased away but after several approaches a persistent female is tolerated on the nest site. Gradually the male's aggressive displays become subdued, and the potential pair start nibbling at each others feathers and at sticks. Once the female has been at the nest site for several hours, mutual preening is frequently followed by copulation. The pair thus established begin coordinated cooperative activities, one bird always guarding the site whilst the other feeds or collects nest material.

Eggs can be laid from January onwards but most first clutches are produced in March. I believe that the timing of egg-laying can be influenced by food supply because in recent years some of the earliest recorded clutches have been laid by birds which fed well at a nearby fish farm. Considering the size of the bird, a heron's eggs are relatively small; averaging about sixty-two grams, less than four percent of the female's weight. They are about the size of hens' eggs but often a bit longer, usually oval and coloured plain blue-green with a few white chalky streaks. They fade rapidly so that the sequence of eggs can be detected by differences in colour. Most clutches are of three, four or five eggs but clutches of six are not uncommon. Incubation takes about twenty-five days for each egg, and begins with the first egg, so by the time the last egg is laid the embryo in the first egg has started to develop. As the young hatches, the parent discards the eggshell over the side of the nest - this is usually the first evidence of hatch. Hatched shells are lined with vascular membranes and contain a creamy deposit of the embryos' waste products, so they are easily distinguished from the remains of broken eggs which have white membranes and are often yolk stained. From the day of hatch you can hear the plaintive squawking of tiny chicks and within a few days this becomes the persistent *chack-chack-chacking* of begging nestlings, a noise that rarely subsides for long over the next two months.

The begging is almost continuous for there seems always to be at least one hungry chick. The eggs hatch at one to two day intervals and the oldest chick may already weigh up to three hundred and fifty grams as the last nestling hatches at about forty-five grams. The parent birds feed the chicks by regurgitation, initially throwing up bits of half-digested fish onto the nest and offering pieces to individual nestlings. The nestlings soon learn where food comes from and whenever they are hungry begin pecking at the parent's bill. This stimulates the production of the lumpy fish 'pâté', which is often taken directly by enthusiastic chicks shoving their bill inside the parent's throat. In the scramble for food the smallest chicks inevitably get least, so they always seem hungry and the begging calls persist. If food is in short supply, the smaller chicks will grow slowly and many of them will die. If all the young in a nest die the adult pair will usually relay in the same nest within two weeks. At least in Scotland most heron pairs seem to rear young eventually although they may have two or three nesting attempts before they succeed. Most pairs produce two or three fledged young; if food is abundant all the nestlings may survive, but broods of five and six are uncommon.

Heron nestlings are beautiful! Newly hatched chicks are tiny, with rubbery pink legs and feet, and an ungainly, large head and beak which rocks unsteadily when raised. The chick's body is covered in grey down except for the belly which is naked and appears green or yellow. The face has short white down and the crown sports long grey and white wisps which stand erect. From about two weeks of age they develop a good covering of feathers on their backs which helps them to retain body heat so they no longer require continual brooding by the parents. At three weeks their wing feathers start growing. By then the nest is getting messy; the spilled food smells a little, and the nest, the adjacent branches, and often the ground below, are covered in 'whitewash'. At five to six weeks the nestlings start to wander out onto adjacent tree branches and by eight weeks they can fly. At this stage they are almost fully grown and look like juveniles, except for the wisps of down still adhering to the feathers, particularly on the head. They remain dependent on their parents for a week or so, returning to the nest to receive their daily rations of warm fish. By then the adults can be commuting ten to twenty kilometres to get food and may only deliver once or twice a day.

Once they leave the vicinity of the colony, juveniles disperse rapidly. They depart in July and August, a time of year when water levels are usually low and fish abundant, so they have ample opportunity to learn how to fish before the autumn. Undoubtedly some never become proficient and the first deaths occur in August. Life is probably tough for most young herons; fishing requires skill, and there is stiff competition for the best sites. The availability of fish can also change unpredictably; a spate might turn an easy 'two fish per hour' fishing stance into an unworkable raging torrent in a matter of hours. The next period of high mortality occurs in October or November, coincidentally with the first cold weather. As described earlier the mortality of young herons varies according to the severity of the weather but overall only about one in five will survive to breeding age. Mature birds have much better prospects and some of them undoubtedly reach their late teens before they die.

I saw my first heron over thirty years ago but did not study them in depth until 1981. There followed six years in which every March, April and May were monopolised by fieldwork in heronries. Most vivid are the memories of laborious, sweaty ascents to nests accompanied by familiar sounds and smells; the persistent clack of begging youngsters, and the reek of conifer resin, guano and the half-digested fish that young herons throw up when alarmed. On wet days everything was smeared in goo and on dry days the dust and conifer needles got to places you wouldn't believe. The odour of heronries accompanied me everywhere adding a new dimension to family living. The car stank: I remember giving a lift to an American hitch-hiker who, within minutes of climbing in, decided he was "on the wrong route". But I enjoyed the study and, given the time and the stamina, I would try it again because grey herons are fascinating birds.

Herons catch fish in shallow water. Their long legs enable them to wade in water up to half a metre deep, and their long neck gives them the reach to strike at prey. They are wary, continually scanning around, but at times fishing demands their whole concentration.

Most herons nest in colonies high up in the treetops. Their nests are built early in the year before the leaves of deciduous trees have emerged. In areas lacking trees herons use whatever elevated sites are available, such as rocky cliffs or, as in this case, the wall of a bothy ruin in the Hebrides.

Herons are monogamous and one bird of the pair continually guards the nest,
eggs or young, whilst the other is collecting nest material or is away foraging.

Newly-hatched heron chicks are covered in grey down, long white wisps standing erect on their crown, and at about two weeks, body feathers start to emerge.

At three to four weeks old, the nestlings anticipate the arrival of their meals of warm fish. On its return to the nest, an adult bird is greeted by begging chicks enthusiastically tugging at the parent's bill to stimulate regurgitation. By this stage the nest is spattered white and reeks of guano and rotten fish.

The eyes are set wide apart and can be directed forward to provide
binocular vision, enabling a heron to judge distance. The eyes can also be directed
downwards to scan an area both ahead of and below the bill whilst keeping the head
motionless. These newly fledged juveniles, still with traces of down on the head,
are naïve fishers and have much to learn if they are to survive.

Grey Heron Conservation

At present grey herons appear to be faring well in most of Europe. From the records available, it appears that over the last fifty years, grey herons have increased almost everywhere and the current population may be at an all time high. If we tally published counts from European countries, between the years 1975 and 1986 the sum total is about fifty-eight thousand breeding pairs. This is probably a substantial underestimate because countries such as Czechoslovakia, Hungary and Russia are not included and there were thousands of herons counted there in the 1950s. Moreover, from the experience of counting heron nests in Britain, we know that even in areas very well covered by competent bird watchers, heronry census counts can under-estimate the number of breeding pairs by at least a third. The overall European population could thus total about a hundred thousand pairs. Britain has about ten percent of these.

In most countries there appeared to be a population decline in the 1960s. In some places this was apparently due to the prolonged cold weather in the winters between 1961 and 1963, but at least in Britain, and probably elsewhere, the sustained low numbers were attributed to pollution from toxic organo-chlorine pesticides. These substances were applied to agricultural land in great volume during the 1960s and were effective pesticides because the toxins were very stable and their effect long lasting. Unfortunately, this persistence also applied to organisms higher up the food chain, where the chemicals became concentrated as they were ingested and stored in fat. Herons are at the top of aquatic food chains and have been shown to accumulate very high levels of residues of the pesticides DDT, Aldrin and Dieldrin. Other, similar substances, such as those collectively known as polychlorinated biphenyls which are used in industry and 'leak' into the environment incidentally, can also accumulate to dangerous levels in herons bodies. These toxic organo-chlorines caused a huge decline in the populations of predatory birds; killing adults, and decreasing the production of young by causing embryo deaths and thinner eggshells which were easily broken as the parents tried to incubate them. Herons were less affected than other predatory birds because they could easily try again if their first breeding attempt failed, and those that bred successfully produced large broods, so there were plenty of potential recruits to replace those adults which died prematurely. Such mechanisms can only partially compensate, however, and it seemed in the 1960s and early 1970s that heron populations were struggling. In Britain levels of organo-chlorine toxins are now very much reduced, though still present in some areas. In Scotland for example, the levels are highest in the tissues of herons feeding on estuaries.

The other major factor affecting heron numbers is human persecution. Grey herons have few natural enemies - not many predators mess about with herons because the outcome can be substantially worse than "a poke in the eye with a pointed stick". I once found six heron legs in a golden eagle eyrie - a bird that had perhaps got the hang of avoiding the pointed end of a heron's bill - but this is unusual. In contrast, large numbers of herons have been killed through human agency. Before legal protection in 1954, herons were killed openly by trapping, poisoning and shooting, as they were often regarded as pests. Heron-killing, though now illegal, continues today, but is localised and occurs in specific situations.

Herons are accused of eating or destroying so many fish that they reduce the fish harvest for human beings. In reality, if herons are guilty of anything it is of exploiting the good fishing opportunities that we create for them. We put small fin tags on wild fish which make them easy for herons to see. On rivers we place obstructions such as weirs, which herons then use to waylay migrant salmon smolts which we are told become vulnerable as they go over the weir on moonlit nights. We introduce thousands of naive hatchery-reared fish into the big wide world and wonder when herons mop them up. Worst of all, we farm fish in shallow ponds, tanks and floating cages that are poorly protected, then label herons and cormorants as "public enemy number one" and "menace from the skies".

In such circumstances, killing herons (or any other fish-eating birds) is no solution. Grey herons are wide ranging birds and they produce young which disperse far. Shooting herons at a fish farm is a never ending task because a poorly-protected concentration of fish will attract herons from great distances. The farm manager has to shoot night and day, and becomes an irritable, baggy-eyed, paranoiac. A huge number of birds have to be killed to reduce damage at a single farm. David Carss' study of herons at fish farms suggested some simple and easy solutions. The first question he asked was whether herons did real economic damage at cage farms. He measured the amount of fish eaten or damaged by herons and showed that it could represent a significant loss to the fish farmer, though small by comparison with other losses due to disease, theft or vandalism. He watched herons at farms for long periods, saw how they were able to reach fish, and devised some simple precautions to enable the farmer to ensure that anti-predator equipment is effective. The simplest and easiest solution at nearly all farms, is to totally exclude herons with netting. This requires some capital outlay and maintenance but this is small compared with the large costs of setting up and running a fish farm, irrespective of the potential losses from an unprotected stock. Most importantly, the benefits of security from heron damage include fewer sleepless nights for the fish farmer, and a less jaundiced view of one of Nature's most adept fishers, the grey heron.

Recommended Reading

The literature on grey herons is prolific but has been most recently reviewed in a book by Claire Voisin, *The Herons of Europe*, published in 1991 by T and A D Poyser, London. If you can find a copy, read the New Naturalist monograph of *The Heron* by Frank A Lowe, published in 1954 by Collins, London, and stuffed with interesting detail. Some of the best heron illustrations I have seen are in Keith Brockie's book *The Silvery Tay*, published in 1988 by J M Dent & Son, London. Finally, detailed advice about heron problems at fish farms, is given by David Carss in the report *Fish Farming and the Scottish Freshwater Environment*, commissioned and published in 1990 by the NCC (now Scottish Natural Heritage).

Herons often feed on the seashore, taking small fishes from among
the seaweed. Such feeding areas are very rich and can sustain an adult heron
every day of the year. However they can only be used at low tide and that
places an upper limit on the amount of fish that can be removed.

Herons gather to roost at a sheltered 'standing ground' near
the breeding colony. Such congregations offer security in numbers for
off-duty breeding birds and immatures. Most herons do not start to breed
before they are two or three years old but they attend colonies in
earlier years, watching the activities of breeders.

Herons are visual predators so they need light by which to fish.
They can be seen foraging at all times of day and on moonlit nights, but
are particularly active early in the morning and late in the evening.

Herons can spend much of their time in feather care. This bird
is exposing its feathers to the heat of the sun, which will straighten the quills
and align the barbs to give 'feather perfect' plumage.

Herons are both agile and majestic. In flight the head and neck
are retracted, the legs held out behind. The broad, rounded wings beat
slowly, almost leisurely, and the flight ends with a prolonged gliding
descent on slightly decurved wings, prior to a gentle landing.

Enjoying Grey Herons

The best way to enjoy birds is simply to watch them going about their business. Watching a heron fishing is as good a spectator sport as you will get anywhere. There is the anticipation as the fish is sought and located, a nail-biting tension as the bird moves into position, and the thrill of success as the fish is caught, or twinge of frustration if it is not.

Look out for herons wherever you go. If you see one in the water it is almost certainly fishing, so try to view the site without disturbing the bird. One of the best places to watch herons fishing is where a road runs along the shore, especially on shallow shelving rocky shores covered in seaweed, particularly the sort with very long yellow fronds studded with bladders (egg wrack). Search the shore for herons fishing when the tide is low and watch. The bird may be alarmed, with head erect and feathers sleeked, but providing you are not too close, it will soon resume fishing. Check whether it is an adult with a white head and neck, or a bird in its first year, with a grey upper mandible. Watch how it shifts its position and its gaze until it locks onto a fish. The body eases slowly forward, and the neck retracts then - splash ! Hit or miss ? Big fish or tiddler ? If the bird missed, how long is it before it finds another fish ? What proportion of strikes are successful ? How long will an unsuccessful bird persist before it gives up and moves to a new location ?

Watch the heron's reactions to other birds. If another heron flies overhead does it call ? If the fishing bird responds by stretching its neck obliquely and pointing its bill upwards, it is giving a public warning. If the intruder comes too close the crest might rise and there could be some aggression. Do intruding youngsters invoke the same sort of reaction as adults ?

Next, try looking at life from the heron's viewpoint - stand still, peering into the water from a bank or from a bridge, or try wading in the water. See how long it takes for fish to re-emerge from hiding. Mark a spot on the stream bed and try to jab it with a stick from above the water's surface - it usually takes some practise.

Finally, if you wish to help monitor grey herons breeding in Britain, take part in the National Heronries Census, organised by the British Trust for Ornithology (The Nunnery, Nunnery Place, Thetford, Norfolk IP24 2PU).

Grey Heron Facts

Other names:

United Kingdom

Shetland	- Haegary, Haigrie, Skip hegrie
North of Scotland	- Craggit heron, Craigie heron (from *craig* = neck)
Tayside	- Herle, Herral, Herald, Erle, Yerle, Tammy herl
Central Scotland	- Craiget heron, Frank (after the call)
Dumfries & Galloway	- Jenny hern, Lang-neckie heron, Craigie crane
Borders	- Hurant, Lang-necket haaran
North of England	- Hernsew, Heron-sue, Jemmy lang-legs, John crane, Yern
Midlands	- Moll hern
Southwest England	- Longie crane
East Anglia	- Harn, Harnsey, Frank
Southeast England	- Jack hern, Frank
Scottish Gaelic	- Corra, Corra-ghritheach
Irish	- Coreisk
Manx	- Coayr glas, Coayr-ny-hastan
Welsh	- Creyr glas, Cregyr, Crechydd
Icelandic	- Grahegri
Norwegian	- Heire
Swedish	- Gra hager
Finnish	- Harmaa haikara
Danish	- Fiskeheejre
German	- Fischreiher
Polish	- Czapla siwa
Russian	- Cepar nanar
Hungarian	- Szurka gem
Dutch	- Blauwe reiger
French	- Heron cendre
Spanish	- Garza real
Portuguese	- Garca real
Italian	- Airone cenerino
Turkish	- Balikci kusu
Scientific name	- *Ardea cinerea*

Races or sub-species:

A. c. jouyi	- China, Korea, Japan, Thailand, Malaya and Indonesia.
A. c. firasa	- Madagascar.
A. c. monicae	- Banc d'Arguin, Mauritania.

Breeding population:

Scotland	- about 3,800 pairs in 1985.
Britain	- about 10,150 pairs in 1985.
Europe	- perhaps 100,000 pairs.

Measurements:

Total length	- 95 to 105 cm
Wingspan	- 175 to 200 cm
Average weight	- male 1500 g, female 1360 g
Weight range	- 800 g (emaciated) to 2300 g (very fat)

Average annual mortality
(estimated from ring returns):
- First year 56%
- Second year 47%
- Older 30%

Breeding in Scotland:

Most herons breed in colonies.

There are often repeated breeding attempts by pairs that fail but only rarely (if ever) is a second brood of young produced in a year.

First year birds frequently attend heronries in spring but there are only a few records of them breeding.

Most birds will be in their second or third year before they start breeding.

Egg size: average of 100 eggs 59.6 x 42.6 mm. (range 46.6 x 36.4 to 66.5 x 43.5 mm.).

Fresh egg weight: average of 39 eggs 62.9 g (range 54.0 g to 70.7 g).

Clutch size: average of 241 clutches 4.09 eggs (range 2 to 8, 95% were 3 to 5 eggs).

Incubation: 25 to 26 days per egg (32 to 33 days per clutch). Both sexes incubate.

Fledging period: 7 to 8 weeks.

Brood size: average of 165 fledged broods 2.33 young (range 1 to 6 young).

Biographical Note

Mick Marquiss started watching birds some years ago as a boy in Northumberland, and is now a professional ornithologist employed by the Institute of Terrestrial Ecology. His studies in Scotland have included work on red grouse, sparrowhawks, ravens, and herons and he is currently investigating the predation of young salmon by red-breasted mergansers and goosanders. By no means a specialist, he is mainly concerned with the influence of land use on the plants and animals of the Scottish countryside.